YOU CAN
Hike Grand Canyon

For anyone who dreamed of doing this but thought it was too late

David Aeilts

The Wordsmith

Minneapolis, Minnesota

Publisher: The Wordsmith, 5809 Hyland Courts Drive, Bloomington, Minnesota 55437, U.S.

ISBN 978-0-9887356-8-2

Library of Congress Control Number 2016906545

First Printing – English Edition

Author's Disclaimer: Hiking Grand Canyon rim-to-river-to-rim is not for everyone, even if you would like to. You'll need your doctor's approval, the dedication to train for an extreme event, and the rich advice freely offered by our National Park Service. Even then you must understand that hiking in the arid, unforgiving wilderness of this great national treasure carries with it significant challenges that this book does not purport to minimize. Hike at your own peril. *See Hiker Tip #1.*

That said, the ideas contained in this brief book should help you succeed, if hiking down and up in one day is your goal. This is how I learned, by listening to the stories of others who have done it.

DEDICATION

To God, who created this marvelous Canyon.

To my friends, who showed me how to enjoy it.

To my wife Nanci, who encourages my Big Adventures.

CONTENTS

INTRODUCTION
You can do it!

Maybe you're like me . . . you're 40, 50 or a little older and you think the opportunity to do certain things has passed you by. YOU are the reason I'm writing a series of books with the theme "You can do it!"

The year before I turned 60, a friend challenged me to hike Grand Canyon rim-to-river-to-rim in one day. A confirmed couch potato and having undergone open heart surgery two years earlier, it would have been easy for me to pass. For some reason, however, I chose to accept the challenge. This book is about my "Big Adventure" as my wife Nanci calls it.

Maybe hiking Grand Canyon is something you always wanted to do but never got around to. Now you think it's too late. Read my story and the tips I offer in these pages for getting ready and actually hiking Grand Canyon. You can do it!

Perhaps hiking the Canyon is not for you. Most likely there is something else you have always wanted to do. This book should offer encouragement that, even later in life, you can still have a "Big Adventure."

David Aeilts

Bloomington, Minnesota

8

Chapter 1

THE ROAD TO THE RIM
A Friend's Challenge Began It All

I remember the conversation well. I was meeting with Jim, a friend who had asked for my help writing a book. It was early October in 2011, and Jim had just returned from hiking Grand Canyon with friends. At age 65, Jim had hiked Grand Canyon 10 times. He told me how beautiful the Canyon was but also how difficult it was to hike.

Almost as an afterthought he said, "Dave, you should come with us next year."

I don't think Jim really expected me to respond. Surprising even myself I replied, "I'd like to do that."

Now, I have never been an outdoorsman—not since Boys Scouts. I have also never been very successful at staying in shape. Over the years, I've taken out several memberships in local fitness clubs only to cancel them in a month or two because I lost interest.

Here was an outdoorsy, fitness-related activity that, for the first time in my adult life, really interested me. Perhaps it attracted me as much for the comradery and the challenge it promised as for the view. Today, I tell people that the panorama stretching out in front of me while hiking Grand Canyon is my number one motivation. But it was different back then.

There were so many strikes against me succeeding at this. For one thing, I was 59 years old, and I did not have much endurance. I had open heart surgery to replace a faulty aortic valve in 2009, and the following year

I had surgery to remove a cancerous prostate. In my occupation as a writer, I spent a lot of time behind the wheel of my car and in front of a computer screen. My chest was falling into my drawers, and I had grown very fond of taking afternoon naps.

Despite all that, I asked Jim to take me up a local ski hill many people use to build endurance for hiking adventures like Grand Canyon. My friend kindly obliged. He showed me how to pace myself, pausing every 100 or 200 feet at the beginning. "The idea," he explained, "is to work up gradually to where you can make it all the way to the top without stopping." Later, my training would involve making several trips up and down the hill without a rest.

Here again, I don't think Jim expected me to hang in there. But for some reason, I did. Those first few trips up and down the hill were killers. I stopped to gasp for breath part way up—wondering whether I would ever be able to make it without a rest. Eventually I did. *See Hiker Tip #2.*

I took a break in my training over the winter and returned to the slopes the following March, as soon as the snow melted. I usually hiked with others, some experienced and some newbies like me. Those of us who had never hiked Grand Canyon listened closely to those who had. We asked them how to train, what kind of gear to bring, how much water to drink, what we would experience in the Canyon, and a hundred other questions. They graciously answered our queries and wetted our appetites with their trove of Grand Canyon stories.

We took very seriously all that we heard from these mentors and tried to act on their advice. After all, these experienced hikers had gone to the Canyon and come back in one piece. They knew how to overcome the challenges we would face.

One time up and down the hill stretched to 4x, 6x and 8x up and down, without stopping. Late in the summer we added backpacks and slowly increased the weight we carried up and down the ski hill. *See Hiker Tips #3, #4 and #5.*

Finally, at the end of September in 2012, each of us flew to Arizona for the actual hike. Some traveled through Phoenix and some through

Las Vegas, Nevada. My hiking partner Pete and I flew into the Flagstaff airport, rented a car, and drove 80 miles northwest to the South Rim of the Canyon. *See Hiker Tip #6.*

The next day, we explored Grand Canyon Village. Standing on the rim, with the panorama of the Canyon stretching before us, a mixture of nervousness and anticipation gripped my heart. We watched a mule train saddle up and head down the Bright Angel Trail. We even descended a few hundred feet on the South Kaibab Trail, to get an idea of the surface on which we would be hiking.

That night, Pete and I met around a campfire with 30 other hikers and their families. Some we knew and some we met for the first time as we feasted on carbohydrates and made plans for the next morning.

A few of the more experienced would hike down the Hermit Trail, whose trailhead is several miles west of the Village. Others planned to leave that very evening and hike the corridor trails of Grand Canyon under a full moon. My group planned a pre-dawn descent on the South Kaibab Trail, which begins just east of the Village.

Having eaten all the spaghetti and garlic bread we could manage, Pete and I headed back to the Maswik Lodge to catch a few hours of sleep. *See Hiker Tips #7 and #8.*

Before dozing off, we set an alarm to wake us in time to catch a 5:00 a.m. hiker bus from the nearby Backcountry Information Center to the South Kaibab Trailhead.

No turning back now.

A Great Pre-Hike Read

While training for your first hike, read *Canyon Crossing: Experiencing Grand Canyon from Rim to Rim* by Seth Muller. This title is available in print or for $9.99 as an Amazon Kindle eBook.

Seth describes Grand Canyon's corridor routes in detail—weaving the history of trail development with his present-day hiking tales. He'll show you what to expect and at the same time whet your appetite for adventure.

Chapter 2

MY GRAND CANYON FIREWALK
South Kaibab Trailhead to Ooh Aah Point

Early that late September morning, 10 intrepid hikers approached the South Rim of Grand Canyon in pitch darkness and started down. Well, perhaps just nine could be described as intrepid. At the time, I felt anxious about my decision. My trail mates, on this trek of what some refer to as the upside-down mountain, ranged in age from 15 to 65. Could I keep up with them?

My goal was to hike Grand Canyon rim-to-river-to-rim in one day. Starting at an elevation of 7,260 feet, I would descend with the others via the South Kaibab Trail to the Bright Angel Campground on the Colorado River—elevation 2,480 feet. After a brief rest at nearby Phantom Ranch, I would climb back to the South Rim via the Bright Angel Trail whose end-point stood 6,860 feet above sea level. I expected to walk almost 18 miles on these two corridor trails that day.

Experienced hikers told me I would travel about twice as fast down as up. We left the South Rim at 5:45 a.m. Depending on how rapidly I hiked, and allowing for rest stops, I hoped to arrive back at the South Rim between 4:00 and 8:00 p.m. that evening. That was my plan.

Our cadre of hikers quickly descended through a series of severe switchbacks known as The Chimney and then headed north. Our headlamps illuminated the five-to-six-foot-wide path bordered on one side by a sheer rock wall and on the other by a steep drop-off. To those of us in the rear, these lamps appeared as tiny, bouncing theatre lights outlining the soft sand trail and guiding us ever downward. *See Hiker Tip #9.*

Dark night yielded to pre-dawn gray. One-by-one we extinguished our lamps and strained to make out the growing vista before us—ridges and craggy buttes rising from a seemingly endless plain which dropped precipitously in the distance. Down we marched to the rhythmic "click, click, click" of our hiking poles. Nervous small talk turned to reverent silence or exclamations of amazement as morning's light intensified, enhancing our ability to appreciate the panorama.

Less than one mile below the trailhead, we reached "Ooh Aah Point" (0.9 trail miles and 600 feet below the trailhead) in plenty of time to witness the sun cresting the Canyon's rim. Light from the rising yellow orb touched the highest elevations and color exploded across the canyon, setting our path on fire.

The beauty of the sunrise assured me that this is where I was meant to be and renewed my confidence that six months of training had prepared me for this day.

Peaks cloaked a moment before in a bluish haze burst into flame as the celestial powerhouse topped the Canyon's rim. Rock strata previously barely distinguishable now blazed with bright yellows and oranges at first and later displayed more subtle gradients.

We stood in wonder at this nearly 360-degree vista, watching a heavenly spectacle unfold. Some hikers stood with mouths ajar—speechless. Others cheered, pointed and exclaimed: "Look at that—no look at that!"

All forgot the weariness of the early morning bus ride to the trailhead and any trepidation we had of hiking at great heights. If our Grand Canyon adventure had ended there, it would have been worth every moment of training; but it continued.

Unmatched Majesty

The Canyon sunrise reminded me of King David's writings, quoted at our campfire the night before. "In the heavens, God has pitched a tent for the sun. It is like a bridegroom coming out of his chamber, like a champion rejoicing to run his course. It rises at one end of the heavens and makes its circuit to the other; nothing is deprived of its warmth." (Psalm 19:4-6 NIV)

Two Corridor Trails

The South Kaibab Trail follows ridges and hugs buttes in its seven-trail-mile, 4,860-foot descent from Yaki Point on the South Rim to the black Kaibab Suspension Bridge on the Colorado River and on to Phantom Ranch. Shade is sparse and there is no water.

The Bright Angel Trail, on the other hand, follows valleys in its nine-trail-mile, 4,380-foot climb to Canyon Village on the South Rim. This trail offers shade and water at several points along the way. *NOTE: This route to the South Rim begins at the crossing of the Silver Suspension Bridge from the Bright Angel Campground and a 1.7 mile hike west along the River Trail to the River Resthouse, where the Bright Angel Trail officially begins.*

Each trail possesses its own unique beauty. For a detailed view of these and other Grand Canyon corridor trails, I recommend National Geographic's trails illustrated topographic map of *Grand Canyon North and South Rims.*

Chapter 3

THE SUN BECOMES AN ADVERSARY
Cedar Ridge to the Tipoff

Less than 15 minutes after topping the rim of Grand Canyon, the sun
began to super-heat the upside-down mountain. Shorts replaced long pants
worn to protect the hikers' legs against 40-degree pre-dawn temperatures.
Those of us with sun shades unfurled them to protect sensitive face and
neck areas, and all slathered exposed skin with sun screen. We began
sucking in earnest on CamelBak® hydration systems and 32-ounce water
bottles to replace fluids being extracted from our bodies.

As opposed to other trails in the Canyon, which follow natural valleys
and streams, the National Park Service built the South Kaibab in the 1920s
along the high places. The view is spectacular, unencumbered by trees and
canyon walls. But extreme exposure to the sun is guaranteed on this seven-
mile-long trail with only two toilet stops, one emergency phone and no
water at any point between the South Rim and the Colorado River.

Leaving Ooh Aah Point, the trail takes a sharp left hand turn back
towards the South Rim before heading north again. The red dirt of this
section of trail, illuminated by the rising sun, made it seem like we were
treading a ribbon of glowing coals.

It can be windy at the rim, but on the morning we hiked the South
Kaibab Trail the air was still, especially as we walked deeper into the
Canyon. I recall hearing little except for our foot-falls and the rhythmic
"click, click, click" of our hiking poles on the trail. Wildlife on the upper
trail consisted of ravens soaring overhead and squirrels darting in and out

of the rocks along the trail, looking for handouts. Lower down, desert lizards clung to rocks at the side of the trail, almost imperceptible as they blended with their surroundings.

We made our second stop about 7:00 a.m. at a rest area on a broad flat plain halfway down the ridge. At Cedar Ridge (1.5 trail miles and 1,140 feet below the trailhead) we sheltered on the north side of a composting toilet, since the scrubby pinion pine trees on that exposed terrain provided little shade. We drank more water and began to consume the trail food we'd brought along. Besides continual hydration, Grand Canyon trekkers must eat regularly. The exertion of the hike could extract up to 500 calories an hour from our bodies, and we didn't want to get behind the nutrition curve. *See Hiker Tips #10 and #11.*

Our informal company of friends, which hung together until sunrise, had begun to spread out. A couple of young dads with 15-year-old boys on a rite-of-passage adventure quickly disappeared down the trail. Of the remaining six hikers, the more experienced stopped for shorter breaks and were generally on the trail before the first-timers. Soon, our tight formation extended and contracted like an accordion over several miles of trail.

We continued down the ridge until we came to O'Neill Butte, an imposing mountain rising from the desert plateau of Grand Canyon. After snaking around the butte's midriff, we walked out on a flat slab of ground 3.0 trail miles and 2,040 feet below the trailhead.

That slab, leading to a precipice called Skeleton Point, overlooked scenes both beautiful and terrible. First the beautiful: a short walk to the left treated us to our initial glimpse of the Colorado River as it snaked through the Inner Gorge of Grand Canyon. Now the terrible: Dead ahead lay the wicked Red and Whites, a nasty set of switchbacks that would lower us another 1,220 feet to a wide desert plateau called the Tonto Platform.

With some trepidation, we surged over the precipice and down this steep zig sag section of the South Kaibab Trail reinforced with timbers and boulders to prevent rainstorms from washing out the trail. These obstacles and the severe incline punished our knees and calves. *See Hiker Tip #12.*

Descending the Reds and Whites, our group got strung out to the point where at least half an hour separated the first and last hikers. Partway down, I stopped at a wider section of trail where I could lean against a large rock for support. Sweat flowing from beneath my hat brim, down the sides of my face, and into the corners of my eyes stung and obscured my vision. I pulled a tan farmers handkerchief out of my pocket, took off my glasses and wiped the salty fluid from my eyes and forehead.

Replacing my glasses, I took a long sip from my drinking tube and made some adjustments to my backpack. Snapping a quick photo of two hikers descending the trail above me, I pocketed my camera and continued on. Two other hikers had already passed me, and I wasn't going to be the last one down the grade.

"Click, click, click . . ." the sound of my hiking poles echoed against the rock wall to the side of the trail. Growing a little weary and having difficulty negotiating this section of trail, I made a mental note: "Take fewer photos and get as rapidly as possible to the next rest stop."

Chapter 4

PLUNGING TO THE BOTTOM
Tipoff to the Inner Gorge

At 8:30 a.m., I hauled myself out onto the Tonto Platform and gratefully dropped my pack at what the Park Service calls The Tipoff. The Tipoff is a rest stop for mule trains headed up the South Kaibab Trail from Phantom Ranch and a staging area for hikers about to enter the Inner Gorge of Grand Canyon. Besides a rail for tying mules to, The Tipoff features the only emergency phone along this seven-mile route from the South Rim to the Bright Angel Campground on the Colorado River.

Already at this hour, the sun's heat and light flooded this flat, waterless rendezvous making the shade on the north side of the compostable toilets a desirable place to sit on a rock, chew some jerky, and drink from my CamelBak® while waiting in line to use the facilities.

The line was long. We'd arrived at The Tipoff at the same time as a 12-mule train coming up from the river. A day earlier, I'd watched the same two mule drivers saddle up their 10 paying customers and head down the Bright Angel Trail for an overnight at Phantom Ranch. Now they were on their way back up. After giving their mounts and butts a rest, the riders would travel the same stretch of trail we'd just come down and arrive at the South Rim well before noon.

Many wince at the thought of swaying on a mule with the edge of a cliff sometimes inches away. The drivers have a saying they hope will allay the fears of prospective riders. "If a mule stumbles, it's all over—but a mule never stumbles." It's definitely another way to see the Canyon, for those who cannot hike or raft.

I listened casually to a conversation between a female rider and a grizzled trail boss with a handlebar moustache. "Are you married?" she inquired. Cinching a saddle on a mule next to her, the trail boss stated without averting his eye from the task: "Ma'am, I've been a cowboy for 40 years." I guess this was all the information he considered necessary for his curious passenger to draw her own conclusion.

On the last 2.6 miles of trail to the Bright Angel Campground, we'd meet another 12-mule train coming up from the river. This string of "long-ears" had also descended the Bright Angel Trail the day before, carrying provisions for the ranger stations and the ranch. Now on its way back to the South Rim, the mules hauled mail that had been stamped "Delivered by Mule at Phantom Ranch—the Bottom of the Grand Canyon." They also carried all the garbage generated by staff and guests at Phantom. Besides helicopters, which are very expensive, there is no other method of moving people and materials from rim to river and back. That is the reason for one hard-and-fast rule enforced by the Park Service: "Whatever you pack into the Canyon, you pack out of the Canyon." *See Hiker Tip #13.*

After resting several minutes at The Tipoff, it was time for our final drop to the bottom of the Canyon via a steeply descending trail. Entering Grand Canyon's Inner Gorge, our party of six hiked down another set of switchbacks followed by a sweeping staircase that took us far west before bringing us back to our objective.

At points along this difficult stretch, we stood on ledges overlooking the Colorado River. We could hear its rushing waters now, but it was still hundreds of feet below. Then we got our first view of the black Kaibab Suspension Bridge where our trail crossed the cold, swift-running river. Down, down we walked; yet the bridge seemed to elude us.

On one switchback, we met the aforementioned mule train climbing the South Kaibab Trail from Phantom Ranch. As the mules neared, each of us backed against the cliff wall. We looked to the mule drivers for direction, as we had been taught. There was none—just a tip of their hats as they passed. Back on the trail, we continued down.

We were getting strung out again, despite the good pace our leaders had set for the black bridge—and Phantom Ranch beyond. We wanted to arrive at the ranch by 10:00 a.m. After a brief rest, four of our group planned to hike the North Kaibab Trail to the North Rim, a distance of 14 trail miles. Pete and I planned to hike the Bright Angel Trail back to the South Rim, a distance of 9.5 trail miles. To avoid hiking a tough set of switchbacks on the Bright Angel Trail during the middle of the day, we intended to leave Phantom no later than 11:00 a.m.

But there was a problem. My friend Pete arrived at Phantom with nausea, a headache and exhaustion. As for me, I did not walk into Phantom Ranch until almost 11:00 o'clock.

I had twisted my right knee as I stepped over one of the timbers placed across the trail to hold it in place. As a novice hiker, I didn't think of changing my stride and leading with my good, left leg. I continued stepping over those logs with my right leg, further aggravating my injury. My descent to the bottom slowed as each log became more painful to cross. Working my way down the final staircase, I had to side-step each timber to manage the pain or look for a way around the end of the log. Both tactics took more time, and I soon fell way behind the pack. *See Hiker Tip #14.*

The experienced hikers in our group had mentored us well. "No hiker leaves another hiker alone" they had stressed during months of preparation for this adventure. Though my progress slowed, I was never abandoned. A guy named Chuck, who I'd met just that morning, stuck with me as I labored down the last set of switchbacks and descended a staircase that might as well have been constructed for giants. Coaching me, encouraging me, and lagging behind our main group with the excuse that he wanted to take more photos, Chuck led me down and across the Colorado River via the black Kaibab Suspension Bridge. In pain, I followed him the last half mile to legendary Phantom Ranch. We had hiked just over seven miles from the South Kaibab Trailhead. *See Hiker Tip #15.*

I arrived at Phantom that September morning with a sore right knee and a blister on the small toe of my left foot. Having trained for six months, I had weathered the steep down-hill hike with only minor pain and inconvenience. Had I not trained, my trip to the bottom of this upside-down mountain may have ended badly. As it was, I was ready for a break.

Prepare, Prepare, Prepare . . .

While each trail in Grand Canyon exhibits its own unique beauty, some present more challenge.

Less-developed trails require more hiking expertise and a Backcountry Permit from the National Park Service. The corridor trails (Bright Angel Trail, South Kaibab Trail and North Kaibab Trail) require no permits for day hiking and offer the greatest degree of security. More developed with more traffic, these Grand Canyon "superhighways" have been equipped with strategically located emergency phones and ranger stations at Cottonwood Campground, Bright Angel Campground and Indian Garden.

The presence of a ranger, however, does not guarantee safe arrival at a destination in this most ruggedly beautiful environment. Nor does sheer physical strength or a young age guarantee a hiker's success. Treks to the bottom of Grand Canyon warrant careful preparation to endure the rigors of the journey and regular intake of fluids and nutrition to avoid dehydration and depletion of energy.

Chapter 5

OASIS IN THE WILDERNESS
Detoured at Phantom Ranch

A friend of mine who has hiked Grand Canyon many times wonders why anyone would stop at Phantom Ranch. "I've been there before and there's just not much new to see," he argues.

Well, not everyone thinks that way. I know hikers who walk Grand Canyon's corridor trails every year who stop each time at this isolated outpost at the bottom of the Canyon. Especially to the first timer, there is a thrill in touching base at Phantom Ranch.

True, if you're not staying at Phantom overnight, you probably want to hurry up the trail. It is also true that there are only a certain number of things you can do at Phantom Ranch if you are hiking through. You can order lemonade or mail a letter at the lodge, to be delivered to the rim by mule. You can also use the toilets and fill up your CamelBak® with water at the faucet in front of the lodge. Additionally, you can soak your feet in the Bright Angel Creek, which I can personally attest feels wonderful. But if you want a meal, you must have ordered it at least a day in advance—and if you intend to grab a last minute bed at the bottom, good luck.

Despite the naysayers, I say "Don't miss Phantom Ranch!" With its rustic appearance and sparse amenities, it's a small slice of paradise to the hurting hiker and is guaranteed to bring a smile to anyone wandering miles from either rim.

The first thing that greeted me as I entered that late September morning was a tall glass of lemonade presented to me by my friend Pete. Downing that sweet-tart treat and sitting in the air-conditioned lodge that functions as a gift shop, a check-in desk and a dining room with the capacity to seat 84, I gained enough strength to think about what needed to be done next.

I walked out of the lodge, stowed my pack under a picnic table, grabbed my first aid supplies and headed for Bright Angel Creek to soak my feet. As soon as I stepped into the cool, swift-flowing water, my early morning handiwork of moleskin and adhesive tape—dyed the color of the trail's red dirt—let loose and floated to the surface. Then I sat on a rock to dry and re-bandage my feet. Pulling my hiking shoes on, I limped back to the lodge, expecting to resume my hike.

But Pete was still feeling nauseous and "headachy". If we left Phantom Ranch now, at 11:30 a.m., we would arrive at the Devil's Corkscrew (the switchbacks I mentioned earlier) at the hottest part of the day.

The experienced hikers in our group advised us to wait until 3:00 p.m. Perhaps Pete would feel better, and we could strike up the Bright Angel Trail with expectations of reaching the Corkscrew after 4:00 p.m. By then, the switchbacks would be in a shadow. So, with the rest of our party headed north, Pete and I decided to extend our stay at Phantom Ranch.

Three o'clock came and my hiking companion felt just as ill as he did earlier in the day. We needed advice, so Pete suggested we visit the ranger station located about 200 feet south of the Phantom Ranch Lodge. The station, a combination office/residence with log walls and a porch, represents the National Park Service at the bottom of the Canyon.

Scott, a ranger temporarily assigned to the Phantom Ranch office, met us at the door and called his boss, Bil Vandergraff, on business-band radio. There is zero cell phone signal at the bottom of the canyon, so communications with the North and South Rim are maintained via wired phone lines and two-way radios.

A 14-year Grand Canyon veteran, Bil Vandergraff said he'd meet us in his office in 10 minutes. We lowered ourselves into two chairs across from his desk and waited, grateful to be in air conditioning. Mid-afternoon temps at Phantom Ranch had peaked at 93° F. that fall day.

True to his word, Bil walked in the door just a few minutes later and shook hands with us. The head ranger, who is also an experienced EMT, began asking Pete questions about his symptoms and how much water he'd drunk on the trail. Pete had actually consumed four liters of water over the seven-mile hike, which was more than I had. Satisfied his intake of water and food had been sufficient, Bil gave his diagnosis.

"I think you've got a little heat exhaustion," he concluded. He also suggested Pete may have eaten some trail food on the way down that did not agree with him. *See Hiker Tips #16 and #17.*

"As I see it, you have two choices," said the ranger, "wait until the sun goes down and then hike up the Bright Angel Trail or stay in the campground tonight and hike out in the morning." Bil said he'd provide us with mattresses, and that we could sleep under the stars. "In any case," he told Pete, "you have to cool down." One way to do that, explained Bil, is to lie in Bright Angel Creek.

The shallow creek, which runs through Phantom Ranch and Bright Angel Campground, joins the Colorado River about half a mile south of the ranch. The Colorado is too cold to bathe in without risking hypothermia, but hikers regularly wade or lay their whole bodies in Bright Angel Creek to cool off and to soothe sore muscles.

"Just a second," said Bil, after giving us this advice. He picked up his phone and called the desk at the Phantom Ranch Lodge. "Do you have anything open for tonight?" he asked. Pausing briefly to listen to the response, Bil looked up at us.

"They've got two bunk beds in the men's dorm," he said adding, "It's air conditioned." "They're $40 per night," the ranger continued. "Do you want them?"

Pete and I looked at each other and answered in unison: "Yes!"

The ranger reserved the two bunk beds under his own name, as well as two steak suppers that evening. We thanked Ranger Bil and hurried up the path to the lodge to pay for those prized accommodations at this wonderful oasis in the desert. Then Pete could begin his cool down process.

Plan Ahead to Stay at the Bottom

It is indeed rare to get a bed at Phantom Ranch without making reservations well beforehand.

A friend of ours called Phantom Ranch after returning home, to see if he could reserve a room for September of the following year. He was told there were no beds available for that period and that they were currently accepting reservations 13 months in advance.

Rooms are usually gone just a few minutes after reservations open. However, there are occasional cancellations and rooms can become available closer to your desired date. Calling or monitoring the Phantom Ranch website may result in a reservation, if your travel plans are flexible.

It's much easier to score a site at one of the three campgrounds along the corridor trails. Reservations for Cottonwood Campground on the North Kaibab Trail, Bright Angel Campground on the Colorado River, and Indian Garden on the Bright Angel Trail open six months in advance and require a backcountry permit from the National Park Service.

Chapter 6

LOOKING UP AT THE RIM
The Fear That Seizes Many a Hiker

After stowing our packs, Pete took a nap in the air-conditioned bunkhouse while I journaled in the dining area at Phantom Ranch Lodge.

A sign on the wall of the lodge expressed the awe I felt as I sat at the bottom of this national treasure which measures up to 18 miles across (as the crow flies) and 277 river miles long, with a depth of one mile. The sign read:

> **Where tranquil trails, turbulent streams,**
> **Mountain monuments and deep ravines**
> **Wind and turn, rise and fall.**
> **God knows best how he made them all—**
> **Rugged lands of the west.**

Later, I took a walking tour of the ranch and sat on a rock while Ranger Scott gave a talk to ranch guests arrayed under a giant cottonwood tree. He spoke about Indian tribes who had farmed at the bottom of the Canyon in the summer and had hunted game at the rim in the winter.

A fascinating speaker, Scott had the undivided attention of the guests, many of whom had come down on foot or by mule with the intention of staying several days at the bottom of this upside-down mountain. A fair number made this pilgrimage every year.

Before the talk ended, I returned to the bunkhouse to wake Pete. At

5:00 p.m., we joined both hikers and mule riders for a steak dinner, served family style with all the fixings. The dinner cost $45 a plate, a testimony to the expense of bringing everything into Phantom Ranch on the back of a pack animal. The food was delicious, and the company was superb as mule drivers shared their tall stores (no doubt many were true) from years spent on the trail.

After dinner, we returned to the bunkhouse in the dark. Pete confided that he felt much better, which gave us both hope for the hike out next morning. Pete's iPhone® showed zero signal at Phantom Ranch, but thankfully the phone's alarm still worked. He agreed to set it for 4:30 a.m., since we'd signed up to eat breakfast during the dining room's 5:00 a.m. slot next morning. After a little conversation with other guests and re-taping my feet, I lay back on my bunk and dozed off.

One piece of advice a seasoned hiker gave me early on was to face down any temptation to panic. "As you are hiking Grand Canyon, especially for the first time," my friend told me, "you will look up and wonder how you are ever going to make it out." He added emphatically, "Resist that thought!"

My experienced friend explained that emotions can easily overwhelm a hiker who gets behind on water or food intake, or who becomes ill. The physical and mental stresses of the hike can combine at the bottom of the Canyon to overwhelm the hiker and make the journey seem impossible. This state of mind and body, called bonking, makes it difficult to go on.

My time of testing came in the middle of the night. I woke with a start at 2:00 a.m. Nine other guys in the bunkhouse at Phantom Ranch slept soundly. I lay there wondering whether my friend Pete had set the alarm of his iPhone correctly. We had to eat breakfast and be on our way by 5:30 a.m. to avoid being punished by direct sunlight on the most exposed sections of the trail.

Whether or not we would wake in time was not the only thing bothering me. I had re-taped my feet the evening before and stuck them under a blanket before falling asleep. Now I could feel the tape pulling away from my skin, and I had no extra tape with which to protect my feet against blisters on long hike back to the South Rim. *See Hiker Tip #18.*

Turning on my right side to reach my socks on the floor, I felt a painful cramp in my right calf muscle. I winced and pulled on the front of my foot to release the cramp. Immediately the same thing happened to my left calf. Exhausted from the pain and not wanting to provoke another cramp, I remained motionless and stared at the bottom of the mattress above me. This was the low point, physically and emotionally, that I'd been warned about.

In my mind, I looked toward the South Rim of Grand Canyon, nine-and-one-half miles away, and murmured, "How am I ever going to make it out of here?" My buddy had heat exhaustion, and I had a bum knee. At two in the morning, things seemed to be going from bad to worse.

Despite these panicky pre-dawn thoughts, I managed to do a few stretching exercises to fend off further cramps. I pulled on my socks to preserve my unraveling tape job and fell into a mercifully deep sleep for another hour or two.

The next thing I heard was the bunkhouse door creaking open and a female voice announcing, "Okay guys, here's your 4:30 a.m. wake-up call."

I guess we didn't need that phone alarm after all.

Chapter 7

YOU WILL WALK OUT
Our Early Morning Launch from Phantom

We threw our legs over the sides of our bunks. Pete and I didn't have to sort through our packs for clothes. We had not planned to sleep at the bottom of the Canyon, so we simply climbed back into yesterday's red-dirt-streaked threads and laced up our hiking shoes.

Then, with flashlights and hiker lamps showing the way, we walked down a short, dark path to the lodge. The warm light from the dining area illuminated the circle in front of the lodge where we waited with the others. No street lights spoiled the ambiance of this remote outpost.

Promptly at 5:00 a.m., a staff member opened the door and invited us inside. Almost all ranch guests eating at this hour were hikers. The mule riders and their minders would eat during a later shift. Servers brought out the breakfast spread, again served family style. We passed the bacon, eggs, pancakes and biscuits up and down the long tables, together with syrup, butter, gravy, hot sauce, milk, orange juice and plenty of coffee.

I ate moderately, not wanting to feel stuffed once we got underway. Pete just picked at his food. As 5:30 neared, the hikers one by one grabbed the bag lunches they'd ordered, adjusted their packs, filled their water containers from the tap in front of the lodge, and struck off down (or up) the trails leading from Phantom Ranch. Pete and I left the dining area and stood under a tree just outside. I sensed something was wrong, but I wasn't prepared for Pete's confession.

"I feel just as nauseous as I did yesterday," he said and headed for the toilet. In a few minutes, Pete was back with a pained expression on his ashen face.

"I don't know what to do," he said, wondering, "Should I stay here another day and wait to feel better?" I didn't know what to do either. Encouraging Pete to head up the trail when he still felt sick didn't sound safe, but what would I do if he decided to remain at Phantom? We had rooms at the rim to check out of and a flight to catch. Should I strike out for the South Rim alone and manage our affairs there, or should I stay with Pete. The phrase "no hiker should be left alone" replayed in my mind.

I was glad when Pete suggested going back to the lodge to talk with Brian, a server who looked like a savvy hiker. Earlier, Brian had told us that one of the reasons he worked at Phantom Ranch was the opportunity it gave him to explore Grand Canyon on his days off.

Inside the dining room, we found Brian clearing away the breakfast dishes. Pete told him our story. He ended with, "I was feeling great last night after dinner, ready to start hiking, but this morning I feel as bad as I did when I got to Phantom Ranch yesterday. What do you suggest?"

Brian looked closely at Pete. "Are your legs in good shape?" he asked. "Yes, they're fine," said Pete. Hearing that, Brian shoved a stack of pancakes and a pitcher of orange juice at Pete. "Eat all you can, even if you don't feel like it, and get on the trail," advised the waiter/hiker firmly. "You will walk out of here."

We decided to take Brian's advice. Pete ate part of a pancake and carried another cake outside, stashing it in his backpack. "I'm going to try," he said with resolve, as he hoisted his pack on his shoulders. "I'll try to make it as far as the Silver Bridge." The bridge is about half a mile from the Bright Angel Campground, which is next door to Phantom Ranch.

Pete and I walked a couple hundred feet along the trail and then stopped to pray. "Lord, we don't know how we're going to do it," I said, mindful of my bum knee as well as Pete's nausea, "but we pray you will help us get back to the rim." We started out again. The time was 5:45 a.m.

The Silver Suspension Bridge is the means by which hikers going up or

34

coming down the Bright Angel Trail cross the Colorado River. The entire water supply for the South Rim also crosses the river through pipes underneath the bridge deck. Mule trains, however, must travel upriver to the black Kaibab Suspension Bridge, which we crossed coming down the South Kaibab Trail. Mules will not cross the Silver Bridge where they can see the rushing water between the slats of the bridge deck. The deck of the Kaibab Bridge is completely covered.

As we strode through the Bright Angel Campground on the path to the Silver Suspension Bridge, the sky grew lighter, and we could anticipate the dawn. A couple hiking behind Pete and me volunteered to take our photo in front of the bridge, and we took theirs.

Then, we crossed the bridge and followed the River Trail along the south side of the Colorado. Pete later told me that he set another goal after reaching the Silver Suspension Bridge. "I'm just going to try to make it to the point where the trail turns away from the Colorado River," he had said to himself.

Part way along that 1.7-mile stretch of River Trail, I saw Pete pull out his iPhone® and begin taking pictures. The sun had cleared the rim and turned some of the higher peaks bright orange. The scene with the light above and the river still in shadow was breathtaking. That's when I knew Pete was feeling better. He was able to focus on something other than his stomach—the magnificence of Grand Canyon at sunrise.

Chapter 8

THE BRIGHT ANGEL TRAIL
Our Road to the South Rim

After crossing the Silver Suspension Bridge to the south bank of the Colorado, Pete and I walked west for about 20 minutes. The sandy path rose a few hundred feet before dipping back almost to the rushing river, losing all of the altitude we'd gained over our mile-long walk downstream. Some refer to that stretch of the River Trail as Heartbreak Hill, but to us it didn't seem that bad. The sun was coming up, and we were making progress on what we knew would be a nine-and-a-half trail mile hike to the South Rim. If we had not gained elevation, we had at least progressed 1.7 trail miles toward our goal by the time we reached Pipe Creek where it empties into the Colorado. At that point, the Bright Angel Trail turns up a side canyon to the south. We turned with it.

The River Resthouse at this junction offers hikers toilets but no water. Here we met a private guide and his two clients. Pete and I stopped briefly to use the facilities and lingered to inspect the design of the building's roof. Across the peak ran a row of spikes designed to discourage birds from roosting there. The guide was replacing some trim hanging off the eaves. "The Park Service tries hard to maintain the trails," he explained, "but it doesn't have enough maintenance crews to be everywhere at once, so I help whenever I can." It was obvious he had taken ownership of one of the trails from which he makes his living.

I say "one of the trails" because the wiry guide, who appeared to be in his upper 50s or lower 60s, informed us that he works as a guide-for-hire in Yellowstone and Jackson Hole as well. On this particular day, he was taking two young Argentine tourists up the Bright Angel Trail. As we eavesdropped, the guide lectured his clients, a young man and a young woman with thick accents, on what they could expect to see along the Bright Angel Trail. In particular, he told them about the California condor, which had been dangerously close to extinction but which is now flourishing in Grand Canyon.

Before moving on, we asked the guide about the trail ahead. He told us we would cross Pipe Creek several times as we headed up the side canyon that draws its name from the stream. "At one point," said the guide, "Garden Creek will merge with Pipe Creek." Garden Creek flows down from Indian Garden, the next rest area on the Bright Angel. There we would find drinking water, toilets, a ranger station and shade.

For the moment, however, Pete and I were focused on a legendary monster situated between us and Indian Garden. "How far is it to the Devil's Corkscrew?" we asked the guide. He told us it would be another 20-30 minutes before we reached this series of severe switchbacks which we hoped to scale before the sun rose too high in the sky. "When you come to a set of big steps, you'll know you've reached the lower end of the Corkscrew," he advised.

Chapter 9

UP PIPE CREEK CANYON
Resthouse to the Base of the Corkscrew

For six months, we'd been hearing about the Devil's Corkscrew, the most challenging section of the Bright Angel Trail which rises 4,380 feet from the Bright Angel Campground to the trailhead on Grand Canyon's South Rim. We'd heard descriptors like "the stairway of the giants" and "caught up in the clouds" applied to this section of trail.

"The Devil's Corkscrew fakes you out," said a veteran hiker, explaining that it will take longer to hike than it appears. "You'll be taking one big step after another and climbing over one rail tie after another, and especially if you're doing this for the first time, it'll take you about an hour to climb."

According to a ranger, the Devil's Corkscrew consists of seven fairly steep switchbacks followed by a wide arching swing upward. From above, said the ranger, it looks like a zig-zag path cut into the side of the rapidly rising cliff by a pirate's sword. The Corkscrew measures a little less than one trail mile in length, and hikers climbing it gain several hundred feet in altitude.

The key to climbing the Devil's Corkscrew, we'd been told, is to hike it in the morning or late in the afternoon. "When the sun is coming up in the east or going down in the west, there are lots of shadows cast by the steep canyon walls," explained our friend, Jim. "But about 2:00 p.m. on a late September afternoon, the sun is overhead and shining directly onto the path." That kind of oppressive heat can sap a hiker's energy. *See Hiker Tip #19.*

On this late September morning, Pete and I had one more good reason to climb the Devil's Corkscrew as early as possible. Pete suffered heat exhaustion the day before and was advised by the rangers at Phantom Ranch to avoid hiking in direct sunlight. So we quickly moved south from the Resthouse on the Colorado River, pushing up Pipe Creek Canyon toward the Corkscrew about a mile distant.

The Bright Angel Trail, which officially starts at the River Resthouse, intersects Pipe Creek several times on the way up the canyon. When we couldn't find rocks to hop across, we had to wade through the ankle-deep stream. Water soaking through my socks immediately released the last of the adhesive tape protecting my feet against blisters. Sloshing out of the stream, I made a mental note to buy waterproof shoes for future hikes.

Following the creek up the canyon, we passed through lush zones of vegetation and saw incredibly beautiful waterfalls. The sun had been up for barely an hour and air temperatures were still in the 70s. Nevertheless, Pete and I stopped briefly every time our trail crossed the creek to soak our hats in the stream and splash water generously on our faces, arms and chests. We did everything we could think of to keep from getting overheated.

Chapter 10

THE GIANT'S STAIR STEPS
Defeating the Devil to Enter the Garden

As the guide promised, we came to some giant stone steps and knew we had arrived at the bottom of the Devil's Corkscrew. We climbed these steps one after another and soon found ourselves treading a series of ramps or switchbacks carved into the side of the cliff. It was amazing, after climbing each section, to look back down at where we'd been.

Sometimes we looked down and saw other hikers on a ramp we'd just climbed. As promised, the climb was steep and there were lots of logs and stones in the trail. Working our way skyward, Pete and I could feel the energy draining from our bodies. We constantly had to wipe dust and sweat from our eyes to see clearly.

My focus on the climb was so intense that I did not realize I had left my fanny pack open. A camera I had borrowed from my generous friend, Gary, slipped out. Thankfully it fell on the trail rather than over the edge of the cliff. I was able to retrieve it, but the incident told me I was a little less stable than I had been on earlier sections of trail. I was using all of my wits to steady myself on the steep incline and ignoring things like securing my gear.

Nevertheless, the views from the Corkscrew were stunning, and we continued to snap photos of the trail above and below us as we wound ever higher.

Despite the rigors of the climb, it amazed us how rapidly the switchbacks fell behind us. Even more amazing and encouraging was a man clad in runner's shorts and a sleeveless shirt who jogged past us half way up the Corkscrew. Obviously running rim-to-river-to-rim that clear day in late September, this 20-something offered the comfort that others shared our trail and could be hailed in an emergency. Pete and I continued on, exiting the sweeping arc at the top of the Corkscrew at about 8:45 a.m.

"That wasn't so bad," we concluded. At the same time, we understood and respected the wisdom of tackling the Devil's Corkscrew early in the morning, when it is cooler and we had more energy, or late afternoon when the sun has moved beyond the rim. At the top of the Corkscrew, we entered a canyon lush with vegetation. From the descriptions given us by more experienced hikers, we knew we were headed straight for the first major rest stop of our morning hike. The rest stop, Indian Garden, lies just 4.8 trail miles from the South Rim. But we were not at the Garden yet.

Pete and I were grateful to have trained for our first hike of Grand Canyon with a group of people who had traveled these trails many times.

"You're gonna come out of the Corkscrew and into this slot canyon with a lot of greenery," our friend Jim had told us. "You'll think you are almost at Indian Garden, but the truth is that you'll still be more than a mile from the rest stop." According to Jim, some beginning hikers have run out of gas after climbing the Devil's Corkscrew, and the thought of having to slog even another few hundred feet is more than they can bear.

For us, the slot canyon and the gently sloping trail at the top of the Corkscrew proved to be a treasure-trove of fascinating rock formations and desert plants thriving on rivulets of water oozing from fissures in the rocks. At this point, Bright Angel Trail follows Garden Creek for most of the distance into Indian Garden. You might even glimpse a big horn sheep or a mule deer along the way.

Our prize that morning was spotting a California condor gliding along the South Rim, which had now become visible since we had hiked our way out of the Inner Gorge. The guide we'd met at the River Resthouse, along with his Argentine charges, had passed us on the Corkscrew. He was now standing to the side of the trail, directing their attention toward the rim where a large black bird moved gracefully back and forth along the face of the cliff. But that was not the only "wildlife" we saw on the way into Indian Garden that morning.

Pete and I also met four 20-somethings headed in the opposite direction. Dressed in black and yellow bumblebee costumes, the two girls led the procession, with antennae bobbing from their heads. *NOTE TO READER: I am not making this up. They whizzed by so fast it didn't even occur to me to take a photo.*

These merry-makers looked so out-of-place that I honestly don't remember how the two guys were dressed. I do remember that one of them carried an iPod with music blaring from an external speaker. They seemed to be out for a morning stroll.

It was ironic that, soon after passing this party group, we observed a sign the Park Service had placed just outside Indian Garden and on the way to the Devil's Corkscrew—where "the bees" were now headed. The sign pictures a fainting figure and warns of dehydration, illness and even death for anyone thinking of hiking from rim-to-river. We pushed on.

Around 10:00 a.m. Saturday morning, we entered what under other circumstances might have been considered a paradise by weary wanderers like Pete and me. After all, we'd taken a 4:30 a.m. wake-up call at Phantom Ranch and had hiked almost five miles with an increase in elevation of 1,300 feet. I wanted to stop and rest, but soon after arriving at Indian Garden, my hiking partner announced his decision to press on to our next destination—the Three-Mile Resthouse.

Chapter 11

THE BEEHIVE
Indian Garden to Three-Mile Resthouse

Pete had good reason to keep walking rather than spending time at Indian Garden, which would be a fascinating place to explore on a future hike. He didn't want a relapse of the heat exhaustion he suffered the previous day on the South Kaibab Trail.

Although the Bright Angel Trail follows the canyons and valleys, giving it more hours in shade, Pete had been advised by Ranger Bil Vandergraff to make the Three-Mile Resthouse his first stop. Between the Garden and the Resthouse was an open stretch of trail that the morning sun would soon flood with potentially dangerous rays. Pete chose wisely to move through that stretch before it was completely inundated with sunshine.

I, on the other hand, was bushed. My knee still hurt from yesterday's hike. Although most of the trail was uphill, favoring the tendons and ligaments I had not injured, even a few feet of descent into a creek bed or stepping over a log on the trail brought a twinge of pain. So at Indian Garden, Pete and I decided to split up. He would continue to the Three-Mile Resthouse, and I would meet him there after I recouped.

To my surprise, after using the toilet, drinking (several times) from the water fountain in the campground, and eating an apple, I felt invigorated. Not wanting to let Pete get too far ahead, I left Indian Garden and headed south on a straight section of trail with a gradual incline. I instinctively looked up at the South Rim of Grand Canyon, clearly visible in front of me.

As I did, I was reminded of what our friend Jim had told us.

"As you leave the Garden, you're going to see a giant beehive sticking to the side of the South Rim," he said. What I would be looking at, explained Jim, is a set of switchbacks between the Mile-and-a-Half Resthouse and the Bright Angel Trailhead.

"You'll scratch your head and say, 'How am I ever going to make it through that thing?' because it looks so amazing," said Jim. "But don't worry—you will!" *See Hiker Tip #20.*

The beehive was just as Jim had described it, but other closer things soon captured my attention. Just 10 minutes out of Indian Garden, I met a mule train with riders headed north and down to Phantom Ranch. I stepped quickly aside as we'd been instructed to do, watching the mule driver for instructions. *See Hiker Tip #21.*

Meanwhile, I slipped my camera out of my pack and began recording video of the procession. The mule driver just tipped her hat at me and nodded, but one of the riders had a request. "Hey, are you taking video?" she yelled. "Will you send me a copy?" Knowing we could not stop the procession to exchange addresses, I simply smiled and moved up the trail.

Looking back on the Garden, as the trail rose toward the South Rim, gave me more opportunities to take video and still photos. A hiker will gain almost 1,000 feet in elevation over the 1.7-mile route from Indian Garden to the Three-Mile Resthouse, so named because of its approximate distance to the Bright Angel Trailhead.

The last several hundred feet of elevation is achieved through a series of switchbacks known as Jacobs Ladder. These switchbacks really make a hiker work for every foot of advance. Unlike the Devil's Corkscrew, however, the hiker exiting Jacobs Ladder receives an almost immediate reward. Right there in the trail is the Three-Mile Resthouse, which offers a roofed picnic area to shelter from the sun, restrooms, and a source of fresh drinking water--except in wintertime.

Greeting me at this hospitable outpost that sunny Saturday morning was the smiling face of my hiking partner, Pete.

Chapter 12

A PROMISE TO STICK TOGETHER
Three-Mile to the Mile-and-a-Half Resthouse

We stopped only briefly at Three-Mile Resthouse. Pete had arrived just a few minutes before me and wanted to stay there a while more. He had not had the rest that I had at Indian Garden. I, on the other hand, was anxious to get back on the trail. We had a noon checkout at the Maswik Lodge and a 4:00 p.m. flight from Flagstaff. I didn't know how long it would take us to hike the last three miles, and I didn't want to miss our flight home.

I told Pete I intended to press on and that he could come when he was ready. What I didn't tell him was that I was fighting exhaustion and that my right knee was still hurting from the day before. I wanted to keep going rather than try to keep up with Pete or any of the other hikers headed for the rim. At this point, I was tired of the adventure, and I just wanted to be alone.

I remember well the wide sweeping curve (up and to the right) that the trail makes from the Three-Mile Resthouse. As I strode up the trail, I looked back down that curve and saw Pete sitting at the entrance to the rest area, munching an apple. That's when my conscience kicked in.

My pledge not to leave a fellow hiker overcame my desire to be alone and nurse my wounds. Pete had kept going while I rested at Indian Garden, but that was because the ranger at Phantom Ranch had advised him to do so. Now, I had no good reason for striking out on my own. About half way up the curve, I stopped, leaned against the cliff wall, and waited for Pete.

Up, up, up we climbed.

Arriving together at the Mile-and-a-Half Resthouse, Pete and I met a family on a day hike to Indian Garden. We overheard the father lecturing his 10-year-old son. Apparently, the boy hadn't drunk at all from the 32-ounce water bottle he had carried from the trailhead, and his dad threatened to stop the hike right then and there if his son refused to replenish his fluids.

Having experienced first-hand the importance of hydrating regularly in this dry environment, Pete and I stopped to lend some support.

"Your dad is right," said Pete. "We've just come from Indian Garden and you won't make it if you don't drink your water regularly."

It was gratifying to see the boy hoist his water bottle at least a couple times after that little lecture and to sense his father's relief.

Chapter 13

JUST A FEW MORE STEPS
To the Top of Bright Angel Trail

From the Mile-and-a-Half Resthouse, we continued up the most expansive part of the Bright Angel Trail. This last section, just under the South Rim, is perhaps the broadest and best maintained, and for good reason. It carries the greatest load of travelers. We met a steady stream of day hikers, many of them just out to stretch their legs on a path which includes a series of switchbacks crossing the sheer rock wall just under the South Rim. Coming out of Indian Garden, it was this final section of the Bright Angel Trail that had looked like a beehive clinging to the cliff.

Fresh from the rim, these day-trippers were talking, laughing and virtually prancing down the incline. Pete and I, on the other hand, were laboring to adjust to the change in altitude (almost a mile above the Colorado River) and were nearing the end of our stamina. But we were also determined to tough it out the last few hundred yards to our goal.

Several things urged us on. At one point, we met an older woman coming down the trail toward us wearing a backpack. As we and she stopped to rest, the woman asked us to guess her age. Without pausing for a response, she informed us that she was 74 years old and was on her way down to Phantom Ranch. "It's my fourteenth year hiking Grand Canyon," she announced.

We also met, on this last stretch of Grand Canyon super highway, a crew of volunteers working to improve the trail. "Thanks for what you are doing," we told them with genuine appreciation.

Then there was a Latin couple who walked the final mile-and-a-half with us, asking about our experiences and sharing theirs. Their company took our minds off our weary bodies and gave us hope that we could conquer this last stretch of the trail. By this time, we were all pausing more frequently. Sometimes they passed us as we stopped to rest, and sometimes we passed them taking a break. Towards the end, all four of us walked together. *See Hiker Tip #22.*

Hikers approaching the Bright Angel Trailhead on the South Rim pass through two tunnels in the rock wall of the cliff. "You'll go through one tunnel and you'll think you're almost to the trailhead," said our friend Jim, before we started. "But you aren't. The second tunnel, a half mile beyond the first, is the real gateway to the South Rim."

Pete and I passed through the first tunnel and came to the second tunnel several minutes later. Our Latin friends took a photo of us in front of the tunnel's archway. They also used Pete's iPhone®, which amazingly still had power after a day-and-a-half off the charger, to photograph us on the last switchback before the trailhead.

In that photo, the famous Kolb Studio juts out from the South Rim just above our heads. We returned the favor by photographing our traveling companions with their camera at the trailhead. Sadly, we never exchanged names or contact information with this man and woman who served as God's hands, lifting us mentally and emotionally to our summit.

At 1:00 p.m., Pete and I reached the trailhead we had visited two days before to watch a mule train start its journey down to Phantom Ranch. Catching our collective breath, we looked back on the road we'd just traveled. Below we spied the Mile-and-a-Half Resthouse and beyond that the Three-Mile Resthouse. In the distance, we glimpsed the path that brought us up from Indian Garden, now a tiny patch of green in the distance.

We had climbed 4,280 feet and walked nine-and-one-half trail miles from the Bright Angel Campground on the Colorado River. Our journey from Phantom Ranch had taken just over seven hours.

As we looked down from the South Rim, it was hard to believe what we'd done. It had been a strenuous, exhausting climb. But after pulling our eyes away from the incredible scene below, Pete and I looked at each other and blurted out together: "We're going to do it again!"

Not for the Faint of Heart

The National Park Service calls Grand Canyon "a powerful and inspiring landscape" that "overwhelms our senses through its immense size." The service labels "adventurous" the visitors who decide to visit the Canyon interior on mules or on foot. Over 200 hikers do require rescue for medical reasons from the Canyon each year.

Due to the journey's rigors, the Park Service reports "first time Grand Canyon hikers tend to react in two ways: either they can't wait to get back, or they swear they'll never do it again." Which will you be?

Chapter 14

NOW IT'S YOUR TURN
To Hike Grand Canyon

Well, I've told you my Grand Canyon story. Pete and I made it down to the river in one day and up to the rim the next morning. The rest of our party made it rim-to-river-to-rim in one day. Your story is yet to be told.

The challenge you will face in deciding to, preparing for and actually hiking the Canyon is to tune out the chorus of nay-sayers who claim you are too old, too sedentary, too urban or too ignorant to attempt this or any other adventure. Especially beware of these voices inside your own head.

Instead, focus on those who faced down similar fears and came away from their first rim-to-river-to-rim hikes with responses like these:

- "My favorite memory is really the whole trip. The spaghetti feed was a great opportunity to meet some of the group before we departed on Friday morning. The scenery, the people you meet on the trail and the accomplishment of finishing are memories I will keep for years to come. The awesomeness and the beauty of the Canyon are hard to describe. I can only say it's worth the trip! It was a 'Grand' experience!"—*Rick L.*

- "I loved the peaceful, quiet beauty of hiking out the last hour or so of Bright Angel, after the sun had set. We had the 'Bright Angel' moon floodlights, as the moon was almost full, although we couldn't yet see it from our point of view down in the Canyon. We walked without head lamps for as long as we could. The insects were in full chorus. The sound of poles, footsteps and breathing was the only other noise. I forgot all about being tired in those serene moments. I initially was a little bummed to think we wouldn't come out before dark. So glad we didn't."—*Julie F.*

- "The entire time in the Canyon was amazing, but I would say my most memorable part was hiking the last hour or two in the dark with close to a full moon. It was such a beautiful evening and a great way to finish the hike. I hope to be back (next year)."—*Pat S.*

- "God's magnificent creation hits one of its exclamation points in the Grand Canyon. It is so large, deep, wide, beautiful and overwhelming, it fills us with awe. We can barely take it all into ourselves."—*Ken B.*

- "This was no small task. It's a pretty big deal to hike the Grand Canyon. It's one of the most difficult things I've ever done and also one of the most gratifying."—*Neal H.*

All of these hikers had moments when they wondered if they had made the right choice. In the end, they concluded they did. As America's poet emeritus Carl Sandburg observed, "Each man sees himself in the Grand Canyon—each one makes his own Canyon before he comes, each brings and carries away his own Canyon." So can you.

Decide today to start down the path to a personal Grand Canyon story. Take both heart and wisdom from the experiences of the people who have contributed to this book. Then begin a Big Adventure of your own.

Prepare thoughtfully. Train diligently. Go confidently. You, too, will look back on your first hike with the satisfaction of having accomplished what only a fraction of visitors each year will attempt. Hopefully, your parting words will be, "I can't wait to come back."

Yes, you can hike Grand Canyon!

Best Resources

You may think you've been reading an expert's manual on how to hike Grand Canyon. Let me be clear. What you are reading is a book of wisdom gained by amateurs who've hiked the corridor trails multiple times, but this is not an exhaustive manual.

To go deeper and keep up with important year-to-year and day-to-day changes in Grand Canyon National Park, consult the real experts. Visit the National Park Service website: http://www.nps.gov/grca/index.htm. Or try a cell phone app like Chiamani.

Appendix A

BEST PRACTICES
For Hiking Grand Canyon

Hiker Tip #1 – The Rim-to-Rim Risk

Like investing in stocks or riding a motorcycle, hiking Grand Canyon rim-to-river-to-rim in one day is a risk you must personally be willing to take.

The Park Service recommends against it, citing the real possibility of dehydration and even death. A handful of hikers do die each year in Grand Canyon.

Have you adequately prepared for the risk? If not, consider overnighting at Cottonwood, Indian Garden or Bright Angel. These campgrounds, with ranger stations, take reservations six months in advance.

If you want the challenge, hiking rim-to-river-to-rim is definitely possible.

Hiker Tip #2 – Pre-Canyon Training

A short rim-to-river-to-rim hike of Grand Canyon involves 18 total trail miles, down the South Kaibab Trail to Phantom Ranch and back up the Bright Angel Trail to the South Rim. At several points, you will hike a grade of more than 15 percent, as you descend 4,780 feet to the Colorado River and climb 4,380 feet to the Bright Angel Trailhead. *NOTE: Hiking North Rim to South Rim involves even greater distances and elevation changes.*

Factors involved in this hike include distance, incline and altitude. Your pre-canyon training should take into account all three.

Hiker Tip #3 – The Right Footwear

Buy new shoes or boots months ahead of the hike. Allow plenty of break-in time. Buy at a brick-and-mortar store with staff trained to fit footwear. Buy waterproof footwear. You will cross streams in the Canyon.

Make sure you can lace the footwear tight enough to keep your heels in the rear. Leave plenty of room in the front. Jamming toes on the descent is a sure way to lose toenails.

Above all, make sure your footwear is comfortable in the showroom. No amount of breaking in will improve the fit.

Hiker Tip #4 – Keep It Real

I train on a ski slope. Walking up and down conditions my body for Grand Canyon inclines, but it is also boring. If my mind wanders or my body hurts, it's easy to imagine I've made more roundtrips than I actually have.

So, I arrange a row of stones at the bottom. These stones represent the number of times I'm planning to hike the hill. I kick one stone each time I complete a circuit. This simple ritual helps me focus and holds me accountable for doing the training I've said I must do.

Hiker Tip #5 – Taper Pre-Hike Training

With three weeks to go, wise Grand Canyon hikers will shorten their training routine.

"Cut training time and distance in half three weeks before a hike and in half again two weeks before," advises my friend Kevin, an experienced marathoner and rim-to-river-to-rim hiker. "This lets the body heal before the big event." Do very little the week of the hike, he adds, but get lots of sleep.

Remember to cut your calorie intake while reducing training. "Some people gain two-to-three pounds the week before a hike simply because they haven't adjusted their eating," Kevin says.

Hiker Tip #6 – Flying to/from the Canyon

Airports at Flagstaff, Las Vegas and Phoenix all serve Grand Canyon. Phoenix's Sky Harbor International (PHX) is 235 miles from Grand Canyon Village on the South Rim. Las Vegas' McCarran International (LAS) is 263 miles from the South Rim. At 84 miles from Grand Canyon Village, Flagstaff's Pulliam Airport is by far the closest airport to the South Rim, although fares to and from FLG will probably exceed fares to and from PHX or LAS.

Las Vegas' McCarren International is the nearest airport to the North Rim.

Hiker Tip #7 – Reserve Early

Several hotels and campgrounds provide lodging options just outside Grand Canyon National Park. For a little more money, you may choose from a variety of hotels or a campground inside the park, in close proximity to the South Rim.

View the choices inside and outside Canyon Village by visiting this website: http://www.nps.gov/grca/planyourvisit/lodging.htm.

North Rim lodging may be found at the same site.

Make reservations as early as possible. Many hotels in and around the North and South Rims fill a year in advance. Phantom Ranch rooms open for booking 13 months in advance, on the first day of each month. All rooms are usually taken in minutes.

Hiker Tip #8 – Pack Right

Remember the wisdom of my friend Jim. "Do everything you can to carry as light a backpack possible. Weight is an enemy on this hike."

My friend Kevin has devised a Top Gear List of five essential items:

1. A CamelBak® with at least 100 oz. of water capacity.
2. Broken-in hiking shoes.
3. Hiking poles.
4. A hat for shade.
5. Trail food you've tried in training.

Other items you may want to bring include foot care supplies, electrolyte powder, headlamps, extra socks, etc. Try to keep your pack under 15 pounds.

Hiker Tip #9 – Lamps and Hiking Poles

Whether starting down a trail before sunrise or returning after dark, you'll appreciate a head lamp (and a spare) to light your path.

As well, poles will come in handy no matter what your age. They'll steady you on steep descents and vault you over obstacles. Even more importantly, they'll take a load off your quads, and they'll conserve your energy in the rarified air near the rim.

Like lamps, poles can be very helpful at night. Hiking the Bright Angel Trail, a friend stuck out his pole and struck nothing. Just in time, he realized he was about to walk off a cliff.

Hiker Tip #10 – Drink Plenty of Water

You cannot completely replenish the bodily fluids you will lose hiking Grand Canyon. The best you can do is manage the loss and avoid severe dehydration.

Most hikers carry 100 oz. CamelBak® water reservoirs in their back packs. Some carry additional 16-32 oz. water bottles.

On the exposed South Kaibab Trail with no water stops, drink the entire 100 oz. reservoir. On the North Kaibab and Bright Angel Trails, consider drinking half a reservoir between water stops.

Always check with the Park Service as to availability of drinkable water at these stops and make sure someone in your group carries a water purification device just in case.

Hiker Tip #11 – Eat Regularly

Like fluids, you'll never replace all the nutrients you lose—only manage them. Consume small snacks of trail mix, energy bars, pretzels, sports chews, etc. at every rest stop. Salty snacks will help you retain water. Eat a bigger meal—something you really like—at the bottom. Eat often, even if you're not hungry.

"Practice eating and drinking while training, so there is NOTHING NEW on the day of your hike," advises Kevin, an experienced Canyon trekker. "The rookie mistake is to bring new foods and drink along without knowing how your stomach will react."

Hiker Tip #12 – Avoid "The Shuffle"

The Kaibab Shuffle identifies hikers who have returned to the South Rim stiff and sore because of the pressure on their legs (specifically the pressure on their quads) from hiking downhill. The South Kaibab Trail, which drops 4,780 feet over a trail distance of seven miles, is notorious for this.

Avoid the Kaibab Shuffle by working out on steep hills before heading to the Canyon. Also train on steps. If you only do flatland training, you will probably get "The Shuffle".

Hiker Tip #13 – Pack In, Pack Out

Whatever goes down must come back up. If you leave anything down there, it will either destroy the pristine nature of the Canyon or it must be hauled out by mule. Mules have enough work transporting guests, supplies and garbage generated by operations at Phantom Ranch.

There are no garbage cans for hikers on the trail or at the ranch, and you cannot throw trash down the toilets.

Plan on bringing EVERYTHING back to the rim again. This includes discarded layers of clothing, food wrappers, and even used tissues.

Hiker Tip #14 – Step Training

Grand Canyon hikers must be prepared to step over logs and rocks strategically placed by maintenance crews to preserve the trail against mule traffic and torrential rainstorms.

Some train for these obstacles by taking stairways instead of elevators. Others prefer the elliptical machines at health clubs.

I train on a flight of 125 wooden steps that rises 80 feet from a creek to a residential neighborhood. Constructed of rail ties, this stairway is a great workout for calf muscles and thighs as well as conditioning the heart and lungs.

Hiker Tip #15 – Avoid Hiking Alone

It is usually better to hike Grand Canyon together. Others lend supplies, marshal help in case of injury or illness, and encourage when the grandeur of these surroundings tempts you to doubt.

Though Grand Canyon's corridor trails are generally highly trafficked, you may not see a soul during the early morning or late evening hours. For this reason, it's best to tackle these trails with at least one other person. An informal group I hike with has a mantra: "No one hikes alone." That's wise.

Hiker Tip #16 – Test, Test, Test

Try everything out before going to the Canyon. If you buy new boots or hiking poles, break them in before you hike. Same goes for a backpack, a hiking lamp, a sunshade or anything else you plan to pack—even the food and drink you will consume.

The bottom of the Canyon is no place to experience the failure of a new hydration system or to learn that the trail mix you're depending on for energy upsets your stomach.

Even if it's non-essential, test it beforehand.

Hiker Tip #17 – How Not to Bonk

If you have problems functioning, and moving ahead with your hike seems incredibly difficult, you are probably bonking. Mentally and physically, you've hit a wall!

Avoid bonking by paying attention to these three areas:

Food—Eat something whenever you stop—even if you are not hungry. *See Hiker Tip #11.*

Water—Dehydration contributes to most rescues. If you wait to drink until you are thirsty, you are already dehydrated. *See Hiker Tip #10.*

Heat—Cover your skin and douse frequently with water. If overheated, stop moving and find some shade. Sit down, drink, eat and cool off. *See Hiker Tip #19.*

Hiker Tip #18 – Focus on Foot Care

Your feet make constant contact with the trail, so it is essential to give priority to their care

Lace your hiking shoes or boots so your heels stay in back. Jamming your feet into the toe boxes is a good way to lose toenails.

Bring moleskin, New Skin®, blister bandages and/or athletic tape in case you develop hot spots. Use as soon as they pop up. Some hikers tape their feet BEFORE they hike.

Bring a change of socks, and soak your feet in creeks along the trail.

Hiker Tip #19 – Managing Heat

Air temperatures warm as you approach the Canyon's bottom. If you hike in late September, as I do, you'll start before dawn at the rim with temperatures of 40-50º F. Expect mid-day temperatures of 80-100º F at the bottom.

At first sign of overheating:

1. SLOW DOWN and pace yourself. This is not a race!
2. Wet a bandana, and place it on your head while hiking.
3. Douse your head with water, or immerse your body in a creek.
4. Still hot? Stop hiking, find shade, or set up a "space blanket" to block the sun's rays.

Wait for evening before resuming.

Hiker Tip #20 – The Mental Challenge

A first-timer may reach the bottom of the Canyon, look up and exclaim: "How will I ever make it out of here?"

Experienced hiker Jim offers this advice. "If we knew everything that will happen to us in the coming year, we would never leave our homes," he says. "But we also understand that by living one day at a time, we can make it and flourish."

"So it is with the Canyon," he adds. "Take one step at a time and you will walk out."

Hiker Tip #21 – Canyon Right-of-Way

Generally, hikers climbing a trail have the right-of-way over hikers descending a trail. The right thing to do, if you are going down, is to stand to the inside of a trail when you meet someone coming up—giving them as much room as possible to pass.

Mule trains transporting people, supplies and garbage up and down the corridor trails have the right-of-way over hikers, who should move to the inside of the trail and look to the mule driver for instructions.

Hiker Tip #22 – Go Slow

Porters guiding hikers up Africa's Mt. Kilimanjaro chant "po-lay, po-lay" (i.e. slowly, slowly) whenever a hiker moves too fast. Hiking slowly prevents exhaustion and maintains a steady pace throughout.

"I decided to follow this wisdom," said my friend Rachel, who has hiked Grand Canyon three times. "I wore a heart monitor and didn't let my rate get above 150."

That was my best hike ever," she adds. "I rarely had to stop and I never gasped for air. My legs didn't burn, and I could easily converse with my fellow hikers."

Appendix B

SOUND TRAINING ADVICE
From an Ex-marathoner

There are a number of approaches for getting yourself in shape for a rim-to-river-to-rim hike, but here are some fundamentals offered by Kevin, a marathoner and veteran Grand Canyon hiker.

- **Start Early.** There is no crash course to whip yourself into shape in the last few weeks of September. Most of us take the summer months to prepare. You don't need to be an Olympic athlete or gym rat to hike the Canyon, but you do need to respect the challenge and train accordingly.

- **Adopt a Time-to-Train Habit.** As a first-time hiker, your starting point should be to make time, beginning in early summer, for training. Shoot for three or more training sessions per week.

- **Gradual Progression.** No need to simulate a whole Canyon hike the first time out. Start small, and then gradually add a bit more challenge and time to each workout. Consistency counts.

- **Hills—The Ups and Downs.** At least one session a week should be hill or stair training. Prepare your body for the descent as well as the climb. Start with 30-45 minutes of going up and down a steep hill or staircase. Add 5-10 minutes each week for 12 weeks. By early September, you should be able to complete a 3-4 hour hill hike session. This is strength training to build your braking muscles (leg quads) for the descent and your climbing muscles (leg hamstrings) for the ascent.

- **Walkabouts.** In addition to focused hill work, the reality of a day crossing Grand Canyon is a day on your feet. It will take about 12 or so hours to cross, and you'll be moving most of the time. If you're hiking North Rim to South Rim, one-third of the day will be spent hiking down, one-third hiking across, and one-third hiking up. Most of us don't spend that much on our feet daily, so dedicate some of your training time to just walking. Using the gradual progression rule, start early summer with a 30-45 minute walk two or three times per week. Then add 10 minutes to the routine every week. This will 'toughen' your feed to avoid blisters on hike day.

- **Bring a Friend.** Be sure to recruit a friend or two to join you in training. Even if they aren't joining you on hike day, it's more fun to have a buddy in training.

- **Ready-Ratio.** No one's perfect in training and most of us miss some of our training days. But you need to be realistic here. If a rookie has completed about 90% of the training described above, he or she is ready for a great day. Less training than that—especially missing the long hill training days—will mean a challenging and painful day at the Canyon.

> You know what they say: "Going down is optional; coming back up is mandatory."

ABOUT THE AUTHOR

David Aeilts is a career journalist, married to one woman for 42 years, a father, a grandfather, and a lifelong Midwesterner. He has worked in agricultural communications for 40+ years. David's goal at 60+ is to explore options for the rest of his life and to finish well. He's currently transitioning from writing for business to writing and publishing stories of transformation. Recent titles include *These Words Changed Everything*, *Broken But Not Forgotten*, *The Art of Transformational Leadership*, and *Refugee for Life*.